This book
belongs to

JOHN DAVIES

THE BATSFORD COLOUR BOOK OF
Shakespeare's Country

Introduction and commentaries by
Garry Hogg

B. T. BATSFORD LTD, London

Acknowledgments

The publishers are grateful to the following for supplying the colour transparencies in this book:

British Tourist Authority page 53; J. Allan Cash page 43; Noel Habgood pages 31, 35, 39, 47, 57, 61, 63; A. F. Kersting pages 33, 37, 41, 55, 59; Kenneth Scowen pages 17, 19, 21, 23, 25, 27, 29, 45, 49, 51.

First published 1976
Text copyright Garry Hogg 1976
Filmset by Servis Filmsetting Ltd, Manchester
Printed by
Lee Fung-Asco Hong Kong
for the publishers B. T. Batsford Ltd of
4 Fitzhardinge Street, London W1H 0AH
ISBN 0 7134 3151 2

Contents

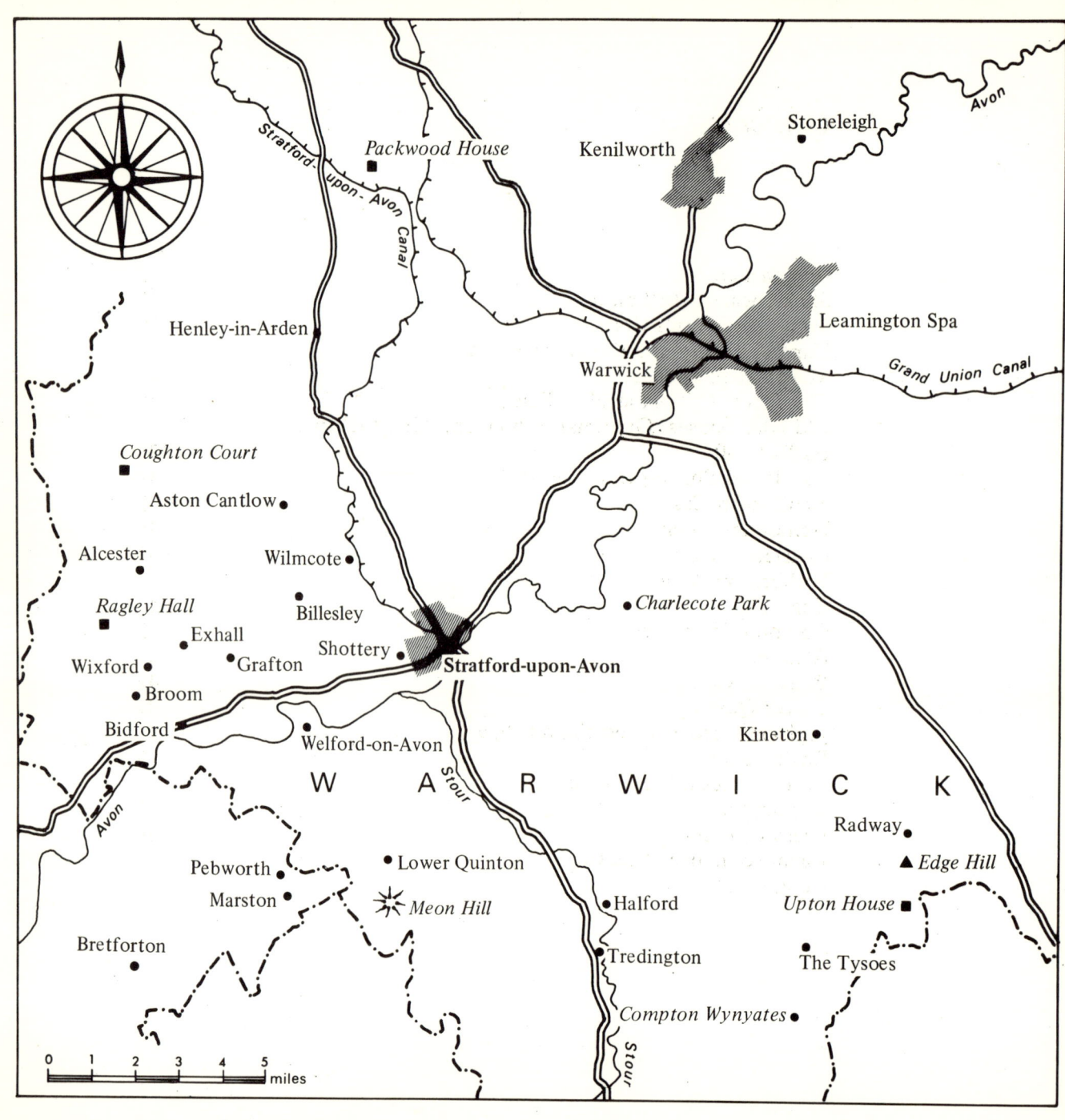

Introduction

Warwickshire may be very truly termed 'The Heart of England'. A line drawn horizontally through it a few miles to the south of the vast urban-industrial sprawl of Birmingham and Coventry shows three counties lying to the east of it and an equal number to the west; twenty-odd counties, inextricably interlocked, lie to the south and again the same number spread out northwards to the Scottish Border. Cartographers estimate (so far as calculations of this sort are practicable in a country so oddly shaped as ours) that the little township of Meriden, just midway between Birmingham and Coventry in the northern part of the county, is the mathematical centre of the country. One or two places within a few miles of Meriden of course dispute this claim; but they have not succeeded in substantiating their own.

Warwickshire, then, is accepted as being, countrywise, the 'heart' of England; it is, however, even more universally recognised as being 'Shakespeare's Country'. For it was in the true heart of this diamond-shaped county, some twenty miles south of Birmingham, that the world's greatest dramatist was born, in Stratford-upon-Avon. If you draw a square, each side of which is twenty miles in length, and with Stratford exactly at its centre, you will find that these four hundred square miles constitute what is generally referred to as 'Shakespeare's Country'. Almost every one of those square miles is in Warwickshire, though a fragment of neighbouring Oxfordshire protrudes into its south-eastern corner and a somewhat longer tongue, the Vale of Evesham in Worcestershire, protrudes into the south-western corner.

The lovely River Avon meanders diagonally across this square from beyond Leamington and Warwick, in the north-eastern corner, through Stratford and on towards Evesham and, eventually, the River Severn beyond the south-western corner. Two branches of the Stratford-upon-

Avon Canal, long since fallen into disuse but now, happily, being rehabilitated by enthusiasts for non-commercial usage, intertwine in the northern half of this square of terrain. There are also a number of small rivers, hardly more than streams – like the Alne and the Arrow, the Leam (which gave Leamington Spa its name) and the Stour and their diminutive tributaries – which add their sparkle to this open landscape of level pasture and ploughland, oak, elm and beech stands, serpentining lanes that link scattered small hamlets one with another – often visible across the wide open fields; and innumerable tracks leading off these to small farms and market gardens lying half-concealed beyond well-trimmed hedges. Though several important roads cut across this twenty-mile-square that we call Shakespeare's Country, and two great cities lie just outside its northern limit, the immediate impression you gain as you diverge from any one of them, in either direction, is that you are entering truly rural England, where time, if it has not actually stood still for several centuries, has at least slowed down to a gentler tempo.

No one could call this a dramatic region. Its highest point, which is to be found near Ilmington, on the border with Gloucestershire, only just tops the 800-foot mark; the fine escarpment named Edge Hill, on the border with Oxfordshire to the south-east, tops the 700-foot mark by less than the height of a man. Indeed, Edge Hill only *seems* so high because of the very low-lying ground immediately to the north, to be approached by one of Warwickshire's very few steep, winding descents. The broad level expanse to which this road (the A422) brings you is the site of the Battle of Edge Hill. A 5-foot cylindrical stone pillar about eighteen inches in diameter stands by the roadside at the foot of the hill; on it is a bronze plaque recording that 'Between here and Radway the Battle of Edge Hill, the first of the Civil War, was fought on Sunday, 23 October 1642. Many of those who lost their lives in the battle are buried three-quarters of a mile to the south of this stone.'

One of Warwickshire's most charming hamlets – and how very many of them there are, with their mellow red brick and snug thatch! – can just be descried on the far side of this battlefield: Radway. It was here

6

that Charles II pitched his royal tent on the eve of the battle. The battle was to rage for no more than three hours on that Sunday in October, but in that time some 5,000 men were killed or so grievously wounded that they had to be abandoned where they lay. That old battle-field today presents an ironic picture: a large flock of sheep graze where soldiers once fought to the death; but they graze amid a network of railway-lines that link the various parts of an extensive ammunitions dump patrolled day and night by guard dogs and overlooked by the military garrison quartered near by. Do these modern soldiers, one wonders, ever feel the presence of Cromwell's and King Charles's men who died here more than three centuries ago? Do the guard dogs' bristles ever rise as they vigilantly patrol these acres during the long hours between darkness and dawn?

Another, and very different, irony lies in the fact that less is known about our greatest dramatic poet, whose name this region bears, than perhaps any comparable figure in the whole of our literary history. It is true that from the content of his plays and sonnets, from the characters he created, from the driving-force implicit within them, we have learned a very great deal about the working of his mind; but so far as hard fact is concerned we still know virtually nothing about him. As with his great predecessor, Geoffrey Chaucer, we know the date on which he died, but we do not know for certain the date of either poet's birth. We do know that Shakespeare was baptised on 26 April, 1564, and it has come to be universally accepted that he was born on 23 April, St George's Day; he died in the town of his birth, on 23 April, 1616, at the age of exactly fifty-two.

What else do we know? That his father, John Shakespeare, was a prosperous tradesman, well respected enough by his fellow townsmen to be elected 'High Bailiff', or Mayor, of Stratford when William was three years old. The boy attended the local Grammar School for a few years, probably leaving at the age of thirteen or fourteen. We know nothing whatsoever of the four or five years between his leaving school and his 'shot-gun marriage' to Anne Hathaway at the age of eighteen; she was some eight years older than he, and already several months gone with child when he married her in November, 1582 – his child, Susanna, who was later to have for brother and sister the twins Judith and Hamnet.

We know nothing of the first years of the marriage. For all the hard, painstaking work put in by scholars down the years we have little to latch on to save an unsubstantiated story that he had to leave Stratford in something of a hurry in order to escape punishment for alleged deer poaching in Charlecote Park. He may have held a temporary post as usher in some Warwickshire school far enough from Stratford for him to be overlooked by the authorities. But this could only have been for a brief while, for he was almost certainly in London within four years of his marriage. Did his wife and children accompany him, or did he leave them behind? If he left them behind, they may have occupied what today is known world-wide as 'Anne Hathaway's Cottage' at Shottery, the cottage that had belonged to her stepmother. Within ten years of his arriving in London he had made money, whereas his father had lost money, and it is believed that the successful son returned, once at any rate, to sort out his financial problems for him. But even this is largely conjecture.

How much, we can ask, too, did 'Shakespeare's Country', as he knew it in his teens, mean to him? One of its outstanding features prior to his day, and even during the seventeenth century, was the Forest of Arden. This was an expanse of oak, elm and beech covering an area some thirteen miles wide by seventeen miles long. It was not thick, impenetrable forest, for the great stands of noble trees were interspersed with farmsteads and holdings and hamlets linked by lanes and set close, as so many of them are to this day, beside the gently flowing rivers and streams. The vast majority of the greater trees have long since been felled – for the building of the many fine half-timbered manor-houses, farms and cottages that are such a feature of this county and neighbouring Worcestershire and Herefordshire to the west; and, less happily, later for the feeding of the furnaces and making of charcoal as the harsh hand of industry spread southwards from Birmingham and the Black Country. In Shakespeare's day much of this region was still

With shadowy forests and with champaigns rich'd,
With plenteous rivers and wide-skirted meads.

The forest, today, is less definably so; but the 'champaigns' – the open country – hardly less. The finest surviving trees are those in the great parklands such as Charlecote. Shakespeare makes specific reference to this forest in the most truly rustic-rural of his plays, *As You Like It,* where nearly a score of scenes are set in the Forest of Arden. The exiled Duke reflects:

Now, my co-mates and brothers in exile,
Hath not old custom made this life more sweet
Than that of painted pomp? Are not these woods
More free from peril than the envious court?

Scene after scene carries the stage-direction: 'Another part of the forest'.

Researchers have sought in vain to establish Shakespeare's identity with the countryside which, as child, boy and youth, he must have come to know; but between-the-lines interpretation, speculation at best, has been the sole result. How different from Wordsworth and the Lake District; how different from Mary Webb and A. E. Housman and the Salopian region that is reflected so continuously in their work, evidence of its impact, which in turn is re-interpreted! And on an even more notable scale, of course, Hardy and his Wessex. The present writer once met, during his own travels, a Hardy enthusiast who was engaged on pinpointing every town, village, hamlet, farm, crossroads, Iron Age camp, stretch of heathland, stream and bridge and field that had been the setting, whether under its true name or thinly-veiled under a Hardy-name, in the whole corpus of the Wessex novels and stories. It was an impressive labour-of-love, for the young man was on foot (as of course he had to be), with a rucksack-full of the novels and a large-scale ordnance survey map of Dorset inked-in with circles and asterisks in green ink. If Thomas Hardy 'put Wessex on the nineteenth-century map', certainly Wessex made Hardy the man and writer he became.

Can the same be said for the man who gave his name to 'Shakespeare's Country'?

Warwickshire is Shakespeare's Country because he was born and died in Stratford-upon-Avon. The villages and hamlets that were established in his day he will almost certainly have known, for a lad of his age would have wandered a good many miles from his home on high days and holidays, on legitimate errands such as taking messages to his father's customers and to his mother's family at Wilmcote; on less legitimate 'errands' such as poaching or fishing in private grounds; in search of accommodating girls, perhaps, in villages far enough from home for him to be able to dally with them without reports being sent back to his father, by now a citizen of some standing in the town. And so on.

There is a handful of unimportant villages whose only claim to distinction lies in the fact that they are included in a piece of doggerel verse attributed (without the slightest authority or even probability) to the Bard of Avon himself. They are:

> *Piping Pebworth, dancing Marston,*
> *Haunting Hillborough, hungry Grafton,*
> *Dodging Exhall, papist Wixford,*
> *Beggarly Broom and drunken Bidford.*

This small cluster of villages may be found just inside the Warwickshire-Worcestershire border, seven or eight miles south-west, west and north-west of Stratford, together with a number of others to which the versifier (whoever he may have been) did not see fit to grant epithets, pejorative or otherwise: North, Middle and South Littleton, for instance; Bretforton, Wickhamford and Church Honeybourne.

Not one of these villages, to which the suggestive epithets were applied, has any outstanding feature. The largest of them, Bidford, is set astride an old Roman road; the ford in its name had been replaced before Shakespeare's day by a shapely stone bridge, the work of the mason-monks based in Alcester, a few miles to the north. But – why 'Drunken'? Local legend has it that Shakespeare the youth went on a drinking bout there with another Warwickshire poet, Michael Drayton. But again this is no more than an apocryphal story; and surely if the epithet were to be used at all, it should be applied to William and Michael? There is even less justification for the epithet applied to Marston. The village appears on the map as Long Marston and has, in addition to its fourteenth-century church, a small building still known as King's Lodge. Here, allegedly, Charles II rested while on the run after his defeat at the Battle of Worcester. He was disguised as a country bumpkin (the story goes), acting as servant to one Jane Lane, and only very narrowly escaped identification. Jane Lane was granted a legacy of £1,000 a year – no mean sum in the middle of the seventeenth century – in recognition of her services.

Wixford perhaps comes nearest to some justification for its epithet, for the whole village was the property of the monks of Evesham, to whom it had been donated by a Saxon earl. It is prettier, too, than some of the others, lying on the bank of the Arrow just before its confluence with the Avon; like Bidford, two miles to the south, it spans the Romans' Ryknild Street which, nearly two thousand years ago, was an important line of communication between Cirencester and Chester, though today much of it can only be picked out by careful work with a large-scale map.

Enough has now been said about these so-called 'Shakespeare's Villages'; the epithets can be dismissed. But each of these villages – like the scores of places of comparable size contained within these four hundred square miles – is worth a visit, if only for the charm of the approach to it along some winding lane that leads to a cluster of modest buildings of mellow red brick, or brick panels inset in rude timber frames usually black with age, or again the pleasing mixture of brick and half-timbering and stone. This last is especially to be found in the southern part of the region, for here we are on the borders of Gloucestershire and Oxfordshire and immediately to the south lie the Cotswolds, whose oolitic limestone-built houses, large and small, are more beautiful, more truly integrated, than those in any area of comparable size in all England – not forgetting the slate-stone of Cumbria.

A different type of stone characterises the area to the east of Stratford-upon-Avon. Russet-hued rather than, as in the Cotswolds generally, ranging from grey to pale gold and honey-coloured in the Oxfordshire villages, this Warwickshire stone has a warmth that immediately catches and holds the eye, whether it forms the fabric of manor-house or farm cottage. It may be said to echo the warm reddish-brown of the soil, as is the case in the even richer red sandstone of Devonshire and in the more subdued tones of the soil overlying the limestone of the Cotswolds. Upper, Middle and Lower Tysoe, with stonework, brick, half-timbering and thatch, a trio of isolated hamlets sheltering beneath the escarpment of Edge Hill, with Radway already mentioned, are as good examples as any of this pleasing blend of traditional building styles. Within a long stone's throw of them, though out of sight in the hollow beneath a high, tree-clad ridge sheltering it from the north, lies perhaps the most mellifluously named and indeed beautifully designed of all the country's Stately Homes: Compton Wynyates.

Warwickshire indeed is unusually rich in these Great Houses of the middle and late medieval period as well as later. Charlecote Park and Packwood House, Ragley Hall and Coughton Court, Upton House and Stoneleigh Abbey are but a few of these. In addition there are the many manor-houses, more often half-timbered than stone-built and in some cases now 'de-moted' to the status of prosperous looking farms efficiently worked by their new owners.

For many visitors to Warwickshire it is in fact the smaller buildings that, curiously enough, tend to leave the dominant impression. (Compton Wynyates, however, must always be excluded, for in itself and in its setting it is uniquely memorable.) Small farmsteads, cottages, inns such as the *King's Head* at Aston Cantlow, facing the medieval guild hall with its jettied upper storey, brick and half-timbering: such buildings as these catch the eye at every turn (and they do not have to be linked with famous names as, for example, Mary Arden's home at Wilmcote is).

The traditional building style hereabouts tends to be rectangular or square panels of brick inset in frames of rough-hewn oak beams; window lintels, as well as those over doorways, are often gently curved – and not by the weight they have had to support down the centuries because usually they are set concave side downwards. Elsewhere you will find a great deal of 'wattle-and-daub' – one of the oldest and most primitive forms of building material; there are good examples of this at Aston Cantlow.

You will also find, in this region that once held vast forests of oak, one of the earliest of building styles: that of the 'cruck frame'. There is an impressive specimen of this in the hamlet of Stoneleigh, in the far north-east corner of this square representing Shakespeare's Country. The so-called 'cruck frame' consists of a curved oak trunk, or large bough, split down the middle and then set up so that the upper ends touch and the butt-ends are well based in the ground. The result is a horseshoe-shaped end-gable that is then reinforced with a lateral beam or two and an outward-curving short beam or two for added rigidity, the whole in-filled with brickwork or, more often, at least in its upper part, with wattle-and-daub. There will be such a cruck frame at each end of the cottage, the two pair of tips linked by a ridge pole from which rafters carry the roof of tile or thatch.

Stoneleigh, in fact, is as charmingly representative a Warwickshire hamlet as you may hope to find: a cluster of mellow stone or brick cottages; a part-Norman russet stone-built church, overlooked by a half-timbered manor-house set amid trees; a row of almshouses with small leaded windows that dates back to the time of Shakespeare; and, to complete an idyllic picture, on a small knoll in the middle of it all, shaded by a flourishing chestnut tree, a smithy. Admittedly this feature of the hamlet is little more than a century old, but it still fulfils its time-long function – which is more than can be said for many traditional smithies today.

The ring of hammer on anvil fills the ambient air; yet there is a serenity about this place (even during playtime at the little school ten yards from it) that is rare to find, these days, and certainly when only a couple of miles separate it from the outskirts of Coventry to the north. Stoneleigh Abbey, alas, has had its day. A few years ago much of the place was burnt out; the part that remains is occupied, but no longer open to visitors; the stabling and other outbuildings seem to be the headquarters of a riding school – perhaps explaining the work in hand at the smithy in the hamlet a mile across the fields; the extensive park-land has been taken over by the National Agricultural Centre and is regularly the setting for the Royal Agricultural Shows.

Nothing, hitherto, has been said about the towns in this area such as, predominantly, Stratford-upon-Avon itself, Leamington, Warwick and Kenilworth – the two last-named of course famous above all for their magnificent castles; there is not space in this Introduction to do more than name them. Guidebooks to them proliferate, and basic information about their chief features will appear in the extended captions that accompany the illustrations. Perhaps Alcester should have been included in the quartet named above, though it is so small a town that it could be regarded just as an overgrown village. Ragley Hall is to be found very close to it indeed. It does contain some of the fine half-timbered buildings, many with the traditional jettied upper storey protruding in medieval style over its pavements. It is this type of building with which one most definitely associates Warwickshire, 'Shakespeare's Country', and it is to be seen in greatest abundance, of course, in Stratford-upon-Avon, birthplace and final resting-place of the Bard of Avon himself.

The Plates

SHAKESPEARE'S BIRTHPLACE

The Mecca of all visitors to Stratford-upon-Avon is of course this house in Henley Street. It was probably less than fifty years old when John Shakespeare bought it, and the greatest possible care has been taken to preserve it substantially as it was when his son William was born there, almost certainly on 23rd April, 1564. The room in which he is believed to have been born is low ceilinged and has a brick and stone fireplace with an unusual mantelpiece.

Only one window overlooks the street, but it is of special interest because a number of literary and theatrical visitors to the shrine have inscribed their names on it: Carlyle, Sir Walter Scott, Sir Henry Irving and Ellen Terry among many others. Care has been taken to ensure that the furniture in the rooms is either that of the owner himself or at least of his period. There is a carved oak chest of Henry VIII's reign, and there are also chairs and stools and what is known as a 'joined' bedstead – *not* the one he allegedly left to his widow. The garden is of interest as well as charm, for it contains at least one specimen of every tree, plant and shrub that is mentioned in the plays. There is also an Ena Harkness rose tree presented by Queen Elizabeth II to commemorate her coronation in 1953.

ANNE HATHAWAY'S COTTAGE

This must surely be the best-known cottage in all England! Its true address is Shottery, but what was once a hamlet has long been absorbed into Stratford-upon-Avon itself, and what was once the home of a yeoman farmer and his family has now been taken over for maintenance by the Shakespeare Birthplace Trust. It continued to be occupied by successive generations of Hathaways for nearly three hundred years after Anne left to marry Shakespeare.

Quite apart from its Shakespearean associations, it is an interesting building in its own right. Much of it dates back well into the fifteenth century, and it is an outstanding example of a modest domestic building of its period. There is some stonework, much half-timbering and in-filling of the traditional wattle-and-daub. If you know where and how to look, you will be able to see a pair of curved timbers known as 'crucks'; these represent one of the earliest methods of building with timber in the country.

When the Trust acquired it, in 1892, it was very carefully restored, and duly filled with furniture of Shakespeare's period. There is an interesting old-style 'courting settle' in the panelled parlour. The dairy has been reconstituted, as also has the buttery. Not the least interesting of the rooms is the well-equipped kitchen with its heavily beamed ceiling.

HARVARD HOUSE AND THE GARRICK INN

Americans have one very good reason for visiting Stratford-upon-Avon, apart from their interest in the world's greatest dramatist. Their Harvard College was endowed by one John Harvard, who had emigrated to America and died there in 1638 – twenty-odd years after Shakespeare's death. Harvard House was John's mother's home before her marriage. For long known as 'The Ancient House', it is a good example of the more ornate style in half-timbering.

It fell into sad neglect but, thanks to the vigorous efforts of a later English writer, Marie Corelli, it was purchased by a Mr Morris of Chicago and duly presented jointly to Harvard College and the United States, whose Stars and Stripes fly from the flagstaff above the lead-paned windows of its jettied main gable. It contains much Elizabethan furniture, Jacobean pewter and other specimens of fine craftsmanship, and during World War Two was used by Americans as a club house. Standing shoulder to shoulder with it is one of Stratford's many famous hostelries, the *Garrick Inn*. This inn is particularly appositely named, for not only was David Garrick a great actor but, in 1769, he was responsible for the first Shakespeare Festival, a commemorative occasion which takes place annually to this day.

MARY ARDEN'S HOUSE

Some five miles north-west of Stratford is another property owned by the Shakespeare Birthplace Trust, Mary Arden's House, in the hamlet of Wilmcote. Like the Hathaways, the Ardens were yeomen farmers, and this sixteenth-century half-timbered building is as representative an example of such a farmhouse as you will find anywhere in Warwickshire. It was the girlhood home of the woman who, in 1557, married John Shakespeare of Stratford-upon-Avon and, seven years later, gave birth to their son William.

The lead-paned dormer windows in the gables look out over an old-fashioned garden. The narrow doorway is low lintelled, set in the timbering, which is simple, strictly functional, rather than ornate. The hall is unexpectedly large for so modest a house, with open fireplaces and a stone floor. As befits a farm, there are outbuildings beside and behind the house. In these, traditional agricultural implements, dairy and domestic utensils and some craftsmen's tools are on display, as in a small rural museum. Not the least interesting of these buildings is a square-built dovecote that contains no fewer than 657 nesting-holes – a reminder that, before the age of deep-freezers, dovecotes were to be found in the grounds of manor-houses, farmhouses and monastic establishments throughout the land.

THE KNOTT GARDEN AT NEW PLACE

One disappointment awaits the visitor to Stratford-upon-Avon: New Place – the house which Shakespeare bought for his retirement when he left London in 1609 and where he lived, and possibly wrote the last of his plays, before his death in 1616 – no longer exists. A few fragments are to be seen on the site, at the corner of Chapel Street and Chapel Lane, parts of the foundations of some walls, a hint of the cellarage, and a well.

Happily, though the house has gone, its gardens survive, having been cherished for many years past so that they now constitute one of the most reposeful corners of all Stratford. The gardens are formal, with well trimmed box hedges and yews. In addition there is an outstanding display of well loved and old-fashioned flowers such as lupins, larkspurs, hollyhocks and Canterbury bells. One feature of special interest is a mulberry tree alleged to have been planted by Shakespeare himself when he took up residence. Close by is the Knott Garden, a replica of a typical Elizabethan garden with raised walks surrounding sunken flower-beds which are 'inter-knotted' – hence the name – and contain most of the herbs mentioned in the plays. The path of crazy-paving is of stone from Wilmcote, the former home of Mary Arden, Shakespeare's mother.

OLD ALMSHOUSES, GRAMMAR SCHOOL AND
GUILD CHAPEL

The stone tower in Church Street is part of the Guild Chapel founded by Robert de Stratford, subsequently Bishop of Chichester, in 1269 for the exclusive use of the Guild of the Holy Cross. There is some fifteenth-century work, but the tower was the gift of Sir Hugh Clopton, who built the fourteen-arched Clopton Bridge over the Avon and also New Place (which Shakespeare bought for his retirement), and who was to become Lord Mayor of London.

Adjoining the church is the half-timbered Guild Hall, dating from 1416. The ground floor served the Guild as administrative headquarters, while the upper floor, known as Big School, became the grammar school. Traditionally, the desk at which Shakespeare sat was by a window in the north wall, though now it is to be seen at his Birthplace. It is probable that travelling companies of players, when touring the district, set up their rudimentary props at the Guild Hall, where the boy Shakespeare would have seen actors for the first time.

The long row of half-timbered almshouses adjoining were established by the Guild in the fifteenth century, and they still provide homes 'for 24 aged local people'. Behind the row of buildings is the 'Pedagogue's House', dating from 1427 and in use to this day.

HALL'S CROFT

This multi-gabled, many chimneyed half-timbered house is seen here across the well-tended walled garden with its shapely sundial. It is just one of the many half-timbered houses which Stratford-upon-Avon possesses in such good measure. Its special interest lies in the fact that it was once occupied by Susanna, Shakespeare's favourite daughter, and her husband, the well-known physician Dr John Hall. It is to be found not far from Holy Trinity Church, where they are buried close beside the dramatist. In the chancel may be seen both the monument to and the gravestone of the Bard of Avon, with the memorable inscription:

Good frend for Jesus sake forbeare
To digg the dust encloased heare;
Blest be ye man yt spares thes stones
And curst be he yt moves my bones.

Hall's Croft is just one of the properties acquired and maintained by the Shakespeare Birthplace Trust. It is a spacious Tudor house, to which certain additions were made in later centuries, though these have married-in well with the original structure. It contains many fine examples of contemporary furniture, and an outstanding fireplace and staircase.

THE ROYAL SHAKESPEARE THEATRE

The original theatre, the Shakespeare Memorial Theatre, built in 1879, was almost completely burnt out in 1926. The present theatre, whose somewhat severe red brick exterior has aroused controversy ever since it was designed by Elizabeth Scott and built in 1932, bears a new name. It could hardly occupy a more perfect site, on the bank of the Avon and set about with trees. And from the theatre-goer's point of view, too, it could hardly be bettered. Its acoustic properties, thanks to what is known as a 'suspended roof', are as perfect as could be. Though the auditorium can seat no fewer than 1,300 people, they are aware of an unexpected sense of compactness and, as it were, intimacy, found usually only in small theatres. The dark panelled walls are in part responsible for this.

The theatre has many modern yet tasteful amenities. These include spacious balconied restaurants immediately overlooking the river, on which there are almost always swans drifting idly by. Close to the theatre is the Royal Shakespeare Theatre Library, together with the Picture Gallery and the Museum. This complex of buildings clearly indicates the variety of interest that awaits the lover of Shakespeare and his works who visits the town, whatever may be his or her specialised inclinations.

KENILWORTH CASTLE

This, of course, is the highly romanticised castle of Sir Walter Scott's novel, *Kenilworth*. Unlike neighbouring Warwick Castle, it is largely ruined. In 1694, Parliament decreed that it should be 'slighted', and this resulted in the virtual destruction of most of the curtain walls and keep. But the ruins here are on the heroic scale, and this view across open fields gives some idea of what it must have looked like before the 'slighting': a complex of massive towers with walls twenty feet thick at the base. The keep measures no less than one hundred feet by seventy-five feet, and all is contained within a perimeter of curtain walls.

There are also the remains of a chapel built by Henry III nearly eight centuries ago, and the remains of a 'pleasaunce' designed expressly for Henry VIII. In fact, Kenilworth came in time to be a castle-palace, and no fewer than five monarchs paid prolonged visits to it down the years. The last of these was Elizabeth I, who brought with her so huge a retinue of Court attendants, and stayed so long, that its then owner, Lord Leicester, was almost completely bankrupted. Seen here in silhouette against the skyline are, most notably, Mortimer's Tower, Lunn's Tower and the oddly named Sainteowe Tower. The containing walls are, most unusually, oval in shape, and attractively framed, now, by stands of trees.

HENLEY-IN-ARDEN

The name of this attractive little market town is a reminder of the forest that once covered so much of the 'Shakespeare Country'. In its High Street, almost a mile long, may be found a surprising variety of architectural styles, including half-timbered buildings. As seen here, the tower of the fifteenth-century Church of St John The Baptist juts out where this narrows; near by is the Guildhall, dating from the same century, and it is here that the High Bailiff is annually elected to office by the ancient Court Leet.

Near by also may be seen what survives of the medieval market cross, generally known as the Butter Cross, where the farmers' wives of the district met to sell their dairy products. Wisely, in view of the ever-increasing Birmingham-bound traffic that flows through this once-quiet little town, the slender cross shaft has been buttressed with wrought-iron supports. It is overlooked by some of the most attractive of all Henley-in-Arden's houses, with lead-paned windows, some rectangular, some diamond patterned, both dormers in the russet-tiled roofs and jettied upper storeys. The little Alne flows by not far away, with Henley's 'twin' village, Beaudesert (locally called 'Belser'), just on the other side of the water.

CHARLECOTE PARK

The house stands set well back in the park from which it somewhat confusingly takes its name. In the park deer still roam and graze among the oaks and beeches as they did in Shakespeare's day when, if persistent tradition is to be accepted, he was caught poaching and obliged to flee the district until the hue and cry had died down. There is known to have been a house on this site eight hundred years ago, but this was replaced four centuries ago by the distinguished family of the Lucys, who were responsible for the magnificent gate house that gives access to the spacious courtyard.

Even since the period of Elizabeth I there has been extensive remodelling of the fabric, and purists may deplore some of this, particularly what was done in the nineteenth century. Yet curiously enough, all seems to blend together pretty well. It is true that the Minstrels Gallery has gone from the Great Hall; but to compensate for this there is still the glorious timbered ceiling. You look upwards at this while standing on a floor of Venetian marble laid down in Tudor times. There are hangings of satin damask on the walls of the Drawing Room, obtained from distant China; and in the Tapestry Room there are Flemish tapestries depicting scenes of the Battle of Edge Hill, in which the Lucys of Charlecote fought on the side of the monarch.

WELFORD–ON–AVON

One of the prettiest of Warwickshire villages, this lies in a loop of the river some five miles downstream from Stratford. True, there are neat houses and bungalows, the country retreats of businessmen and their families, but much of the village is surprisingly unspoiled. Its small church is approached by way of one of the oldest lych-gates in the county, and possesses some features dating from Norman times.

The older part of the village, seen here, with its thatched cottages each with an apron of smooth turf backed by flowering shrubs, spreads across a gentle slope from the water. One is conscious that the village is aware of its innate beauty, and prepared to conserve this. Tradition is strong, and symbolised by the presence of a particularly fine maypole set at the centre of a small, artificially raised green just opposite the general store. It is a permanent installation, striped like the old-time barber's pole and surmounted by a golden ball and a weathervane in the form of a fox being chased. The maypole comes into its own every May Day.

Down near the water's edge is the popular inn, the *Four Alls*, its signboard portraying King, Parson, Soldier and Farmer, and a somewhat cryptic verse suggesting that without the last-named, none of the others would be in existence.

EDGE HILL

This outstanding ridge, over 700 feet above sea level, is a rare feature for Warwickshire. It runs close to the county's south-eastern border, with Oxfordshire and Northamptonshire immediately to the east. The view shown here is eastwards, over good farming country, but the steeper slope, on the other side, drops to the plain on which the Battle of Edge Hill was fought on 23rd October, 1642. Here some 14,000 Royalists faced some 10,000 Parliamentarians led by Robert Devereux, 3rd Earl of Essex. Though the battle raged for less than four hours, at least 5,000 men were killed or too sorely wounded to be carried away when the battle came to its inconclusive end that Sunday afternoon.

Tradition has it that King Charles I watched the battle in progress from a vantage-point on the ridge that is marked today by an impressive battlemented octagonal tower known as Radway Tower, or Castle. This was built a century later by an amateur architect, Sanderson Miller. It is now the *Castle Inn*, and contains relics of the battle in the form of weapons and armour retrieved from beneath the turf of the old battle-field on which was fought a battle that, though bloody and indecisive, marked the commencement of the Civil War.

COMPTON WYNYATES

It is perhaps invidious to say that any one Great House is the most beautiful, and perfectly sited, of all that grace the English landscape. Yet here the temptation is hard to resist. No other, surely, fits more aptly into its setting. The tree-clad hill slopes gently upwards behind it, topped by a windmill; the foreground is occupied by ornamental gardens in which, as at Packwood House, topiary work is among their most distinctive features.

This is the country seat of the Marquess of Northampton, and has been in the same family for eight hundred years. The building you see now, of russet-red brick with stone quoins, was built in the Tudor period. Henry VIII stayed here more than once, and one of the bedchambers is named after him; in it, a window bears the emblem of the king, and also of Katharine of Aragon. The porch bears an inscription in Latin: 'My Lord King Henry VIII'.

Notable as are the great mullioned windows, the dormers, the castellation and the great sundial, perhaps the most memorable individual feature is the array of ornate chimneys, no two of them identical, every one of them a masterpiece of the bricklayer's craftsmanship. Some of them can be seen here, silhouetted clearly against the massed trees behind them.

ALCESTER

This little market town lies on the western fringe of Shakespeare's Country. Its name shows that it started as a Roman settlement, on the River Alne. It stands at the junction of two once-important Roman roads, one of these being Ryknild Street. The Romans called it Alauna. In Saxon times it was a township of some importance; in medieval times it had become even more important, as its many fine half-timbered buildings make abundantly clear. Like Henley-in-Arden, it still has its Court Leet, in which for the past seven hundred years the High Bailiff has been annually elected to office.

But though its timber-framed buildings are noteworthy, perhaps even more so are the buildings that replaced or were added to them in the late seventeenth and eighteenth centuries. There is a fine group of these, Georgian in conception and style, facing the east end of St Nicholas Church in High Street. Though much of this church was rebuilt in Victorian-Gothic style, it has a fifteenth-century door and a thirteenth-century tower. The Georgian buildings are remarkable for the finely proportioned bow and bay windows and the neatly placed dormers. The contrast between the medieval and the eighteenth century is well shown in this picture of one of Alcester's many inns and the half-timbered houses beyond.

WARWICK CASTLE

This viewpoint, on a bridge spanning the Avon, offers perhaps the finest impression of this magnificent castle. Soaring above the great curtain walls are the two main towers, Caesar's and Guy's. Their castellations rise to some 150 feet above river level. Both date from the fourteenth century, and there is a grim dungeon hewn out of the solid rock on which the first named tower is based. The castle was built immediately after the Norman Conquest, on a site still known as Ethelfleda's Mound, after the Saxon 'Lady of Mercia'.

Largely because it has been continuously occupied ever since it was built, it remains, after nine long centuries, in an excellent state of preservation. Successive owners – notably the Beauchamps in the fourteenth century – enlarged and elaborated it, building the formidable barbican, gate tower and curtain walls; but it had already been made virtually impregnable by the first Earls of Warwick during the Baronial Wars. For the past two hundred years it has been occupied by descendants of those early Warwicks, who have preserved and restored where necessary, so that it now ranks among the finest castles in the land. Among its notable and unusual features on a smaller scale is the medieval bear-baiting pit; there are very few indeed of these to be seen in England today.

LOWER QUINTON

There are two Quintons, Upper and Lower, just off the A46 a few miles south of Stratford. Upper Quinton is largely spoiled by the presence of a garrison, but its twin is very attractive, with its village green overlooked by the Church of St Swithun. Its quite modern windows are unusually interesting in that they portray in stained glass a pageant of local history and also the choices of subjects suggested by the village schoolchildren of half a century ago who were invited to put forward ideas for inclusion. They chose, as rural children would, birds and butterflies and insects with which they were familiar. In addition, they demanded some fairy-like figures emerging from their snail-shell homes – a nice touch.

Across the green, standing out among the charming stone-built and half-timbered cottages, is the village inn, the *College Arms*, with its elaborately painted signboard facing it on an oaken post. It bears the arms of Magdalen College, Oxford: 'Lozengry Sable and Ermine and a chief Sable charged with three garden lillies Proper'. The site belongs to the college, and was a gift to Lower Quinton from no less a personage than Henry VIII himself four centuries ago. The inn combines Cotswold-style windows and a neat tile-gabled porch.

JEPHSON GARDENS, LEAMINGTON SPA

By contrast with Stratford-upon-Avon this is a very new town indeed, almost all its buildings being Georgian, Regency, or later. It reached the zenith of its popularity in the late eighteenth and early nineteenth centuries, when, as at Buxton and Matlock, it became fashionable to 'take the waters'. No one did more to develop the place as a spa than a local physician, Dr Henry Jephson. It was he who, in 1838, officially received Queen Victoria, and thus obtained the title 'Royal' on behalf of the town.

Appropriately, the authorities paid tribute to him by laying out on the banks of the Leam, from which the spa takes its name, spacious gardens. This was in 1875, and in fact was one of the first projects of the kind in England, for until that date gardens, like parkland, were the prerogative of the wealthy landowners with stately homes. The bright, clean-flowing river lends a touch of liveliness to the quietude that generally prevails. There is an artificial lake, complete with a small island, a wide spread of water-lilies and water-fowl paddling among them. Another feature of the Gardens is a classic-style 'Corinthian Temple'. Within, again appropriately enough, there is a statue to the worthy individual who did so much to place Leamington firmly on the map.

RAGLEY HALL

Seen on the far side of its terraced gardens, this Great House may not immediately strike you as outstanding; there is perhaps something too rectangular, too uncompromising, about its façade. But do not be put off, for it is rich in treasures large and small. Not the least of these is the imposing classic portico, less old by just one hundred years than the original building, which dates from the seventeenth century. It has been the country seat of the Marquess of Hertford from the beginning, and has been continuously occupied by the same family ever since.

The interior is certainly more memorable than the exterior, save perhaps for the portico. The chief show-piece is without question the superb medallion in the ceiling of the Great Hall. But there is also the very fine Library, which contains thousands of handsomely leather-bound and tooled volumes. The Marquess will tell you that it is his favourite room, and no wonder. There are also the Blue Drawing Room, the Red Saloon, and the Prince Regent's Bedchamber with its huge four-poster bed. In every room there are treasures on display: pictures, porcelain, silverware, glassware, furniture alike reveal the perseverance of successive generations of the family in accumulating *objets d'art*.

LORD LEYCESTER'S HOSPITAL

This is among the most interesting as well as beautiful of all the county's medieval buildings. Dating from 1123, it has had a chequered career. It was originally the Guild House of St George. By 1383 it had become the property of the Guilds of the Holy Trinity and the Virgin Mary. In 1571, Robert Dudley, Earl of Leicester, reorganised it as a hospice, or almshouse, to accommodate a Master, together with 'twelve men or brethren hurt in the wars'.

Though there was an interval during which the building was occupied by the King's School, it duly reverted to its earlier use. The Master, and twelve brethren, all of whom must be pensioners from the Services, either aged or disabled or both, live out their last years in peace, as do the better-known pensioners in London's Chelsea Hospital. Each member has his own small bedroom, sitting-room, kitchen and bath-toom. On special occasions they wear the uniform originally designed for them: an Elizabethan 'gowne of blew cloth', an Elizabethan-style hat, a cloak, and a scarf with a silver badge in the form of the Warwick-shire bear and 'ragged staff'. The men are always proud to show the visitor round the Banqueting Hall, the old kitchen (now a little museum), and the peaceful Inner Courtyard shown in the photograph.

TREDINGTON

The village lies in a crook of the Stour some eight miles south-east of Stratford, just off the main road. There is more stonework here than farther north, for the Cotswolds, with their plentiful oolitic limestone, lie not far to the south. Indeed, this could be taken for a Cotswold village. It is dominated by the beautifully proportioned spire of its church, dedicated to St Gregory, in which there is some indisputable Saxon work still to be seen.

One most unusual feature is the evidence in part of its main walls that originally the door sills were substantially higher from ground-level than they are today. Expert opinion holds that this was designed as a means whereby the Saxon inhabitants could more easily find sanctuary from the marauding Danes. There is a parallel to this in the Irish *clochteachs*.

In this village there was born a baby who grew up to become Admiral Sir Hyde Parker. The name may not be immediately familiar to you, but in fact it was he who, commanding the British fleet at the Battle of Copenhagen, issued the signal to which Horatio Lord Nelson deliberately 'turned a blind eye'. He thus at one and the same time was largely responsible for achieving a great naval victory, and bequeathing to posterity a most useful phrase.

PACKWOOD HOUSE

One of the smaller of the county's many Great Houses, Packwood is best known for its famous yew tree garden, planted in such a way as to represent the tradition of the Sermon on the Mount, the Apostles, the Evangelists, and Christ the Master. They were planted three centuries ago, and have been carefully tended ever since. Now that the National Trust has acquired the place, both house and gardens should be maintained in a fine state of preservation for the foreseeable future. Not the least of its attractions is the fact that it is set in what little remains of the original Forest of Arden.

The main structure, dating from the mid-sixteenth century, is of timber, seen at its best in the Great Hall, which is notable for its oak-beamed ceiling of cruck-style timbers, complete with Minstrels Gallery. In the mullioned windows of the Dining Room are some particularly fine specimens of seventeenth-century Flemish glass, and the Inner Hall is hung with exquisite tapestries, while the Drawing Room has an impressive display of elegant Charles II and Queen Anne furniture. However, in spite of all these riches, it is almost certainly the exterior of stone and mellow brickwork, seen from the Sermon on the Mount Garden, that you will recall from your visit with the keenest pleasure.

CANAL SCENE NEAR STOCKTON

The Stratford-upon-Avon Canal was constructed at the close of the eighteenth century, but fell into disuse with the coming of the railways. After years of dedicated labour, part of it was reopened, to pleasure traffic, at a ceremony performed by the Queen Mother in 1964. Ten years later she ceremonially opened a further section, to the north of Stratford, again for the use of pleasure boats. With its towpath and small bridges, it offers a chance to explore the county by boat or on foot, at one's leisure, in peace. The National Trust will ensure that this lovely waterway is never again permitted to become derelict.

In the north-east corner of Warwickshire, passing through Warwick and Leamington Spa, there is a short stretch of our major canal, the Grand Union (formerly the Grand Junction), which links London with Birmingham and the Midlands generally. It is of course still used commercially (though pleasure boats may also use it). Even as near to Birmingham as this, there are picturesque stretches. The one in the photograph shows a reach of the Grand Union between Stockton and Leamington: a typical surviving canal-side inn, a working 'narrow boat' and a former narrow boat converted for the purpose of pleasure cruising in comfort.

COUGHTON COURT

This has been the country seat of the Throckmortons for very nearly six hundred years. Though it stands close to the main A435 Birmingham road, it is happily screened from the traffic by an avenue of splendid elm trees planted almost a century ago. Perfectly framed between the two lines of trees is the glorious gate house, multi-turreted and elaborately castellated and, originally, accessible only by way of a drawbridge over the moat that has now been filled in. The gate house dates from 1509, and the superbly proportioned wings flanking it, though built two centuries later, match the older part of the fabric perfectly.

The gate house opens on to an outstandingly beautiful courtyard, with gardens beyond it, and on either side the wings of the house contain the main rooms, in every one of which there is some treasure that demands more than a passing glance. The Dole Gate of a convent, for instance, of which an early Throckmorton was abbess; a chair constructed of timber salvaged from the bed in which Richard III slept on the night before Bosworth Field. It was, incidentally, beneath this roof that the Gunpowder Plot conspirators' wives forgathered to await news of the success (or failure) of the attempt to blow up Parliament in 1605.